85 Poems

Gavin Ewart

Hutchinson
London

This edition first published in 1993 by Hutchinson
Reprinted 1993

Random House UK Limited
20 Vauxhall Bridge Road, London SW1V 2SA

Random House Australia (Pty) Ltd
20 Alfred Street, Milsons Point, Sydney, NSW 2061, Australia

Random House New Zealand Ltd
18 Poland Road, Glenfield, Auckland 10, New Zealand

Random House South Africa (Pty) Ltd
PO Box 337, Bergvlei, 2012, South Africa

A CIP catalogue record for this book is available from the British Library.

ISBN 0 09 177541 8

Set in Times by Edna A. Moore, 📐 Tek-Art, Addiscombe, Croydon, Surrey
Printed and bound in Great Britain by Cox & Wyman Ltd, Reading

Random House UK Limited Reg. No. 954009

Acknowledgements

Some of the poems in this book have appeared in the following periodicals, and to them acknowledgements are due: *Ambit*, *Letters* (Royal Society of Literature), *Light* (USA), *London Magazine*, *New Democrat*, *PN Review*, *Poetry Review*, *Raritan* (USA), *River City* (Memphis State University, USA), *Thames Poetry*, *The Auden Society Newsletter*, the *Guardian*, the *London Review of Books*, the *Observer*, the *Spectator*, *The Times Literary Supplement (TLS)*.

For Martin Bax and Alan Brownjohn
with affection

'And we heard the distant and random gun
That the foe was sullenly firing'

Contents

Part Two: 'Frivolous'

Part One: 'Serious'

Elfrida

'Yet why not say what happened?' – *Robert Lowell*

This may be a long mumbling sort of poem,
perhaps because it's the sort of subject that inspires a long
    mumbling sort of poem.
It's about my first cousin Elfrida, whose father
was the black sheep of his family, a failed medical student,
    the kind of father
who in those days (the Twenties) might have been sent to
    Australia.
As a matter of fact (to seek his fortune) he *was* sent to
    Australia.
His father, Sir George, was a very prominent surgeon
who ran the Naval Hospital at Chatham, as a prominent
    surgeon,
in World War I. For this he was knighted.
But poor old George, the son, never looked like being
    knighted.
He failed in Australia too, and came back to be a car
    salesman.
He had once been a Captain in the infantry; but he turned
    into a car salesman.

In 1914, before the War, he had married a Norwegian –
some kind of Scandinavian, she was Swedish or Norwegian –
and she had died in childbirth. So just one child, Elfrida,
about two years older than me, my first cousin Elfrida.
While my Uncle George was busy seeking his fortune
her grandfather Sir George looked after her – a piece of
    good fortune,
you might think. Board, lodging, a Nanny. And he spoiled
    her rotten.
That was the trouble, he really spoiled her rotten.
Baby could do no wrong. And George, her father, was in
    permanent disgrace,

11

the only son to survive the War and a failure and disgrace.
I don't think he often even saw her. Her grandfather was
easily little-finger-twisted.
She must have learned quite early how he could be little-
finger-twisted.
In her teens, later, it would be 'Babs, is that make-up?'
'Oh, no, G.R.!' Lipstick, rouge, she was smothered in make-
up,
quite unacceptable in Hove for an upper class young lady,
but she could deny, his sight was bad, a quite confident
young lady.

There were two brothers, G.R. and E.B. G.R. Turner
played rugger for England
(later Sir George). I'm not sure whether Edward played
rugger for England;
but he was a cyclist, a very famous athlete, fastest thing on
wheels
in the days when a tricycle was the fastest thing on wheels.
So it was 'G.R.' Nobody called him, latterly, anything else.
I would never have thought of calling him anything else.
One summer holiday, let's say in 1924, when I was about 8,
at Wincanton
we stayed in a rented house. It's famous for racing, of
course, Wincanton.
But I knew nothing about horses, about Wincanton or
Somerset.
There were myself, my two sisters, my cousin Richard, and
Elfrida, there in Somerset.
There were good tall straight trees to climb and a big garden
to play in;
Elfrida had been in Italy, in gardens children didn't play in.
We had bicycles, we had hide-and-seek, it was all quite jolly
but one day something happened that wasn't very jolly.
I was mad keen on collecting (and who at that age wouldn't
be?) butterflies and moths,

for me they were sacrosanct, all butterflies and moths,
I also loved the flamboyant hawk moth caterpillars
with their exotic camouflage; now, alas, such caterpillars,
with the clearing of building land and the vanishing of
    nettles,
are hard to find. Peacocks, Red Admirals – the nettles
fed the woolly bears, their attractive larval stage.
All such were stars that filled my rustic stage.

Brimstone butterflies, that lovely yellow! Now only white,
the only rare survivor is the common Cabbage White.
Where are the Death's Head Hawk Moths and the fine Red
    Underwings,
the Swallowtails with their Gothic lacy underwings?
Where are the Painted Ladies and the hawk moths of the
    evening?

But this was daylight crime, it wasn't in the evening.
Elfrida stamped on a woolly bear that was trying to cross
    the path.
She stamped on it and killed it as it tried to cross the path.
I was outraged and furious. I shouted 'That's a Peacock!'
But she had no remorse, though she'd surely killed a
    Peacock.
'No, it's not,' she cried. 'It's a very poisonous worm!'
Perhaps for the peasants of Bordighera, it might be a
    poisonous worm.
In retrospect, I see, she was misled by adult wisdom.
But I was too indignant to be swayed by any wisdom.
There were tears and shouts and tantrums.
Did my mother soothe the tantrums?
Did she say 'Elfrida didn't mean to do it'?
I'm afraid that I assumed that she *did* mean to do it –
my attitude was simply 'Ignorance is no excuse'.
My father was away, on a grouse moor, an excuse
not to be there with the family, and a change from August
    London.

He loved shooting, he was good at it. From a hot and sticky
    London
he escaped. So my mother was the adult
who had to coax a child to behave more like an adult.

Next time (my memory says) that I was with Elfrida
(she was a pretty little girl, blonde hair, blue eyes, Elfrida –
when she was young she was like every little girl in a
    Victorian picture
with her arms round the neck of a big dog – you know the
    kind of picture)
I did indeed behave like an adult. I was fifteen, as I
    remember,
staying in the flat in Hove, as I remember.
I put my fingers on her thigh and pushed up past her
    knickers –
I was experimental, not romantic, with my fingers in her
    knickers –
there were no kisses, close embraces, or lying warm 'I love
    yous'.
She didn't mind too much, though she gave me no 'I love
    yous'.
and knew that she was doing something wrong – we both
    were careful,
my grandfather or the Nanny (you had to be quite careful)
could pop in at any moment. She was hot and wet. Like
    voyages
of discovery, we embarked. Yes, it was like Cook's voyages;
but, on a later visit, everything was different.
I met some of her friends, and the attitude was different.
One or two girls who were dirty-talking raffish,
upper class Hove but with dirty-talking raffish,
trying to impress me, I think, the 'sophisticated' Londoner –
or so they might have thought me, public schoolboy,
    Londoner.
One was a big bold girl, venturesome and handsome
(seventeen? eighteen?) but never shy, and handsome;

14

she had saloon bar jokes – one of an Alsatian,
of a girl who thought she'd 'try her luck' with an Alsatian.
That 'try her luck' was 'have a fuck' I didn't realise –
but sex with dogs, I'd heard of that, and I did realise
that naughtiness and dirtiness, for her, meant sophistication.
They had this primitive, 'provincial' sophistication.
One girl was Rozzie Scrope. G.R., as a historian,
said her family was old (he knew, as a historian)
and that an Archbishop Scrope had been around with Queen
Elizabeth
(is he in one of Shakespeare's plays?) Pronounced Scroop.
Well, Queen Elizabeth

gave her, in my grandfather's eyes, a certain cachet.
I didn't find her very exciting. But that's the point, with a
cachet,
it either works or it doesn't. Weakly snobbish, I thought.
My grandfather
loved titles too. I felt a bit ashamed of a grandfather
who corresponded with Max Beerbohm but always talked of
him
as 'Sir Max' (not 'Beerbohm') whenever he talked of him.
What did they write about? I'm sure they had nothing in
common.
I would have thought Beerbohm would have thought him
rather common.
He wasn't a very good writer. One book on Mary, Queen of
Scots –
Forgotten Forgeries, the Casket Letters and Mary, Queen of
Scots –
and one book of autobiography, *Unorthodox Reminiscences*,
a work of very conventional old boy reminiscences.
And one novel, never published, really terrible stuff,
(that my Aunt Edith tried to edit). I was shown it. Terrible
stuff,
with a very strong didactic slant, about a Countess at Oxford
who went about giving VD to all the lovely young men at
Oxford

(I don't think she meant to); anyway, it was a moral tale
warning of VD. He gave it me to read, as a moral tale
that might yet save the up and coming generation.
My cousin had to read it too (he was the same generation).
The typescript was appalling, and more like *Finnegans Wake*
than almost anything I'd ever seen except *Finnegans Wake*.
I didn't envy my aunt. Neither of his books had a very good
    press.
Once there was a photograph of him with King George V, in
    the local press.
Because he didn't think the photo did him justice
he pasted in a better one, that he thought did him justice.
He was, in fact, a very good-looking man. He must have
    looked magnificent.
In one photo of the England rugger team 'mean, moody and
    magnificent'
is exactly what he is (was it Jane Russell?). This was the last
    'Twenty',
the team that played Scotland in 1877, the last official
    Twenty
before they made it Fifteen and took away some
    forwards . . .

Looking backwards is almost as hard as looking forwards.
A lot of this looks like rubbishing my grandfather.
He might have been a bully and conceited, but as a
    grandfather
he was always very nice to me. He loved children.
My mother told me how he would always talk to babies and
    very young children . . .

I can't remember when I saw Elfrida last before the War;
but certainly, during or after (memory is puzzled by any
    kind of war)
she married Stephen. They both lived in a gin bottle.
What they had in common came out of a gin bottle;
she did once have a governess, but she was more or less
    uneducated.

Cigarettes and gin, but otherwise uneducated.
She wasn't nasty ever, but just terrifically silly,
(you could almost call it a vice, she was so amazingly silly!)
a kind of middle-class equivalent of a Conservative skinhead.
But more pretentious and much more snobbish than any
skinhead.
Because of the Hove aristocracy, she got presented at Court.
(I'm sure my grandfather too wanted the presentation at
Court.)
Stephen was the male equivalent, a rentier with an income
that paid for the gin. When there wasn't sufficient income
she used to pester my Aunt Edith and my mother
to break a Trust that had been set up (my mother
and my Aunt were the Trustees) to keep her from spending
everything on gin – that's how I see it – spending
everything in the Sir George Robertson Turner Trust
which gave her a small income from investment. Trust
her, they didn't. Probably on some predatory raid on London
I saw her again – a flying visit to London,
to argue for more money; it was not a social visit.
Estranged from her father, arguing with aunts, it was not a
social visit.
Later, my cousin and I were made trustees, to replace the old
ones.
'Don't ever let her break the Trust!' was the wisdom of the
old ones.
This was firmly implanted in our minds. Stephen and she
were set
on living in the style of their Silly Conservative set.

When I heard of her again it was all of fifty years.
My aunt, my mother, dead. Stephen dead. Fifty full years!
I had a letter from a Social Worker in Southend,
to say that she was 'very poorly' in the Hospital at Southend
(when did she leave Hove, I wonder? But another wonder
was how she could live for 75 years – and that *was* a
wonder!).

I was the nearest available next-of-kin; but still I didn't visit
  her.
She'd been cut off for so long. Should I have gone to visit
  her?
For years and years she'd had the isolation that she wanted –
she'd certainly had the isolation that she'd wanted!
I didn't go, and if at all my conscience pricked me
this was because of the sharp memory that pricked me
of a stupid pretty little girl stamping on a caterpillar
in days when we were quite as innocent as any caterpillar
with regard to the taste of gin – and much more beside this.
But to go would have been false sentiment, I did think this.
She wanted to be apart, we had never been close, she hadn't
  asked for me.
It would have been different if she'd actually asked for me.
But what gave me pause was the little girl in the garden.

Adam and Eve, and Evil, together in the Garden!
In a week or two she died. No will. The few belongings
had to be collected; in a plastic bag, the few belongings.
There were papers and legalities. We saw the Social Worker,
nice, competent – would Elfrida's friends despise a Social
  Worker?
I thought to myself. Insufficiently One of Us?
But, like Elfrida, the Social Worker valued someone who was
  One of Us.
The Social Worker said she'd been a grand old lady
with her cigarettes and telly; they thought her a real lady
(gin wasn't mentioned much) with her good life stories
of being presented at Court in days before the War, stories
which made a lot of Sir George, and even of a poet,
are you the cousin that she spoke of, are you the poet?
Everyone in the Hospital knew she was an old-style lady,
they all loved her. One of her visitors was a capital-L lady,
who came every week especially to see her, not a local.
But the Social Worker liked her (and she was local).
So she had a kind of Court, in the General Hospital –

innocent, snobbish, silly, in the General Hospital –
till the time was come to fulfil the Death Certificate.
It was a rectal carcinoma on the death certificate.

An Arundel Tomb Revisited

('Their supine stationary voyage')

When we lie in the bed like an Arundel tomb,
stretched out beside each other like those two others
in the famous poem, one takes the hand of the other
(though we are living, and we're not an Arundel tomb):

it's because I love you and you love me –
however you define love, which of course has degrees,
everything everywhere exists in different degrees.
And it's certainly certain that Time doesn't love me

or you or anyone that's born of a woman.
Our faces alter, we get vague with pre-senile dementia,
with hesitating steps towards genuine senile dementia,
where what is what and where is where escapes each man
    and woman.

So this bed, like the tomb, is a ship – as Larkin said –
sailing onward into time, but not to Eternity.
There will be a landfall long before Eternity,
in the hostile sea of Time – as Larkin said.

The War Song of Lewis Carroll

I saw my little son without his head,
I saw the tortured and I saw the dead –
'Why, this is most peculiar!' I said.

I saw the burns, I saw the festered feet
of refugees with nothing left to eat.
'It's a solution, but not very neat!'

was all that came into my mind to say.
I watched the TV bombing every day –
that's the best war, the television way.

I saw the Kurds sent back without their cocks,
their eyeballs in their hands, no feet, no socks –
I said: 'This isn't very orthodox!'

'All war reporting is a monstrous cod!'
cried some. Some left a lot to God.
It seemed to me, in logic, very odd!

'It's quite extreme!' I yelled, 'mathematics men
would not believe it! It's a crowing hen –
and only fit for Cambridge – frightful fen!'

A General said it was a turkey shoot.
The convoys were quite fried – the men, the loot.
'A Victory?' I said. 'The point is moot.'

And some divines said men made earth a Hell –
that made my Anglo-Saxon pride both pout and swell.
I can't deny, they did it very well.

Imperial War Museum

Here, let us say, all war is sanitised –
the question of the *product* isn't raised.
It's like a factory where clean machines
hint at well-ordered past production lines.
The guns stand silent in their lovely paint
and it is innocent air at which they point.

There are no shells scream witchlike as they ride
or charred black corpses on the Basra road.
There's camouflage, and razor wire and scrim –
but not the wounded or the dying scream.
War was imperial, even now it's royal.
Some bodies here would make it much more real!

Some glorious wounds, to frighten or amaze
(some mustard gas would not come much amiss),
some arms and legs, perhaps a severed head?
To reconstruct what History likes hid,
waxworks could re-create the grievous harms
that are not seen in television homes.

This is the War that time cannot corrode,
the Fly-Past and the Victory Parade.
Sadness and Pride, of course, are in the cast –
but no true indication of the cost.
Bring on the war-struck, dazed, the dim civilians!
They should be here, the mild maltreated millions.

15 November 1991

21

Only the Long Bones

'The head gardener happened to be there that day, and I
told him how my husband was first buried at Bawli Bazaar,
then transferred to Maungdaw and after that to Akyab and
finally to Taukkyan. It was distressing to think of these
graves being disturbed so often. Very patiently he explained
the policy of the War Graves Commission and of course I
could well understand why. "But how was it possible? What
remains?" "Only the long bones, Madam, only the long
bones."' – *Gweno Lewis, wife of the poet Alun Lewis, dead
in Burma, 1944*

Only the long bones, Madam, only the very long bones,
we skip the fingers and toes – but we do remember the ribs –
of Lewis and Morgan and Jones.
Knuckle-bones, useful for dibs,
are given to prep school boys.
They're not much use to his nibs!

Only the long bones, Madam, only the very long bones.
Necklaces (fingers and toes) – you could sell them in a bazaar –
anguish I hear in your tones . . .
does it matter *where* they are?
Since most of him is here,
and you have come so far!

Only the long bones, Madam, only the very long bones,
all of them labelled and packed – and the backbone counts
   as long
(I thought you'd like to know that).
Move and bury. It isn't wrong.
It's the way the War Graves work.
It's a game, like Bezique or Mah-Jongg!

The Battle of the Somme

(1st July 1916. 20,000 men killed in one day)

Our barrage lasted for a week.
Their wire will all be gone, they said.
(Such noise we couldn't think or speak.)
You can just simply go ahead!
Just walk, no need to run!, they said.
(We had one lad of seventeen.
He thought he'd had enough. *He* ran.
They shot him, military and mean.)

But in deep bunkers Fritz lay hid,
even in one a double bed.
They manned machine-guns; yes, they did.
And mowed us down like standing stalks.

Don't listen when a General talks!

The Counting Out

(i.m. Roy Fuller, d. 27th September 1991)

Writers old and writers new
have a time and have a cue,
every girl and every boy
ends like Sylvia, Tom or Roy.

Counting out is in the song,
can be short or can be long.
They dance round but they all know
in the end they have to go.

Young ones happy in the sun
have their fling and have their fun
turning in the three times three –
till they stop – and out goes *he!*

Raise a tune and raise a shout,
we are in the counting out;
eyes and ears and stiffened joints,
we go when the finger points!

'Entrance and Exit Wounds Are Silvered Clean'

– Robert Graves

And was there love? Who knows? There must have been.
Although hot love, like war, has gone away –
entrance and exit wounds are silvered clean.

Those girls wrong-ended, telescoped, are seen
as tiny figures on a distant day;
entrance and exit wounds are silvered clean.

They're like old movies on a pre-war screen,
gesturing in eternal black and white.
Entrance and exit wounds are silvered clean

and cause no pain – they're only scars, I mean,
tokens of love's once urgent active bite;
entrance and exit wounds are silvered clean.

Dead Cats

Of course when you see
the little furry bodies lying in the gutter
you mourn for them slightly –

knocked out by a car!
You don't want to think of them too soppily –
nor take it too lightly . . .

And many cats, like cars,
have had just one careful and loving owner.
One such was Miss Olden,

bent double by old age,
deaf, part-blind; that age is *not* the age that
people once called Golden . . .

Her cat was housebound;
and so, as a matter of fact, was she – high
on a high floor of a big block of apartments –

locked into Loneliness,
if you think of life as a large department store,
or a drawer with separate compartments.

Her shopping was done
(and this included cat food, naturally)
by a Welfare worker or a neighbour,

an act of kindness – found
equally among Republicans and Democrats,
those who vote Conservative, *and* Labour.

Natural kindness isn't political.
Her little cat, fed only on cheap tins of cat food,
was never very healthy;

he never looked like the cats
that bounce about in all the commercials,
or the well-groomed cats of the wealthy.

His life wasn't much fun
compared to the lives of the free-ranging cats
that have the run of a garden,

who even get into woods,
gallop over fields, and generally go native
in a local Forest of Arden.

Far, then, from cats called 'feral'
(but perhaps he liked the seclusion – you can't tell –
all happiness is comparative),

he aged and sickened.
At last, he disappeared. Miss Olden called –
but he didn't come. At this point in the narrative

we must recognise
how heart-riving it can be for the owner
when a pet goes missing,

it's as bad, or almost as bad,
as the nothing that takes the place of a lost lover
when petting and kissing

come to a dead full-stop.
Miss Olden was distracted; she called in the neighbour.
He searched everywhere in the flat. Lying

stiff and cold under her bed,
he found him. Where, searching for the final seclusion,
he had been quietly dying . . .

Miss Olden was unwilling to believe

that he was dead – from her deafness she spoke:
'He's only sleeping'.

She asked the neighbour
to tuck him up in his basket, his face showing.
Like a last flame leaping,

hope flared in her thoughts –
'In case he wakes up . . .', she said. A bit mental
you'd have certainly thought her –

or, you could say, in this case,
she hadn't profited from lessons experience
might (and should) have taught her.

The neighbour tucked him up.
He knew he was dealing with a shut mind,
one completely closed off.

And, next day, after quite a long argument,
he succeeded in carrying the cat off to the vet
(£15) to be disposed of . . .

Karen Price

(A Triumph for the BBC's Crimewatch)

15½ and 'in care' since the age of ten.
A great runaway and hanger-round-Cardiff-Bus-Station.
She and Alison were both run as teenage prostitutes
by a lad in his twenties, a bouncer at a night club.

She can hardly have thought he would make her

the unwilling companion of blow-fly grubs,
flesh-eating beetles and ('after at least 5 years')
the host of woodlice and others.

But so it turned out. She was strangled and wrapped in a
   carpet
and buried in the garden, with the help of an Asian assistant
(himself only 15). Alison was there when it happened.
It sounds, in a way, accidental. Her death wasn't intended.
The younger boy went for Alison, the bouncer attacked
   Karen.
Because they both refused to pose, for lesbian photography.

So nine years passed; till some pipe-layers, chance-led,
   unearthed her.

A clever chap, from her skull, reconstructed her face.
Somebody somewhere, at a Police Station, recognised the
   reconstruction –
so next they had a name, and very soon a photograph.
It was there on TV. The Asian lad, watching with friends,
cried out 'Why, I know that girl!' He must have been feeble-
   minded.
Because a friend phoned the Police. They found Alison.
   They found the killer.

The killer was now 31, but steadfast in every denial.
Though he did admit he'd lived there, in the basement flat,
and he recognised the off-cut from the carpet . . .

The way all the bits fitted in was really very pretty.
Something all the crime buffs could really get their teeth into –
they don't mind munching up the beetles and maggots and
   earthworms.
An old skeleton is just an exciting puzzle . . .

But what about the parents? 'In care since the age of ten'.
No girl, no person, would want that as an epitaph, surely?

The Smile, in April 1991

Graham Greene, who died a few days ago, says somewhere
(I can't remember which book)
how the smile in the brothel parlour
could only be given by a *woman* –
no man could ever rustle up that fake-enticing look.

But what about *male* brothel parlours? Eh?
I bet *they* are full of deceit!
It's true, in the old days the female
had to please the male; as a woman,
her talking had to be subservient and sweet . . .

But no more. The truly bright liberated woman
can give a really dirty look
to any man she might encounter . . .
full of distrust and deep hatred –
the kind of look a lobster might venomously give a cook!

Talking to Women

When the dog has had his day,
conversations with old women come his way,
and they're never stuck for something to say . . .

one has a very interesting disease
that affects everything except her knees;
its Latin name is easy to forget, it sounds Chinese . . .

another loads her children with praise,
you'd think she was the Creator, the Ancient of Days;
her Manny is going through a very interesting phase,

and everybody is knocked sideways by Liz
as she rises like a star on benighted showbiz.
No husband is mentioned, the credit isn't his,

but absolutely certainly *hers*.
Like a big talking cat she sits there and purrs.
Naturally, a long-time wearer of natural furs . . .

Another, who has rather better looks,
for years has been writing unpublishable books –
young male literati eat most of the meals that *she* cooks.

She tells you about her latest writer's block,
with gesturing hands above an expensive frock –
you have to swallow the thought 'What a lot of cock!'

This is the kind of thing, hour after hour,
you have to sit through; they have mesmeric power –
they're the Enchantresses, you're the peasant in the
   bower . . .

You couldn't say that they were liars,
but they're all very dedicated self-justifiers
and in the self-praise stakes quite eminent high-flyers . . .

A Short Discursive Whitmanesque on Felix Holt

'"I only came to ask Mr Holt if he would look at my watch
for me," said Esther, entering and blushing a general rose-
colour.' – George Eliot, *Felix Holt, the Radical*.

Esther Lyon is a beautiful ladylike young woman, of doubtful parentage,

not at all unlike Esther Summerson in Dickens's *Bleak House*.

Perhaps all beautiful ladylike young women of doubtful parentage

tended to be called Esther? We have no statistics.

Felix Holt is a big bold intellectual working man, like Joe Gargery with brains,

with good-looking grey eyes, a searching intellect, and virtue.

In order to save his mother from a life selling his dead father's patent medicines,

'Elixirs' which depend on faith and some very dubious ingredients,

he has come to Treby Magna to work with his big hands and support her.

He, in spite of the size of his hands, has chosen watch-mending.

The mother is a bit silly, a pious Dissenter, and neither here nor there,

but a big nuisance to Felix because he wears an open-necked shirt

and in every respect dresses and behaves like a workman . . .

Esther is the putative daughter of a very theological Dissenting Minister –

nobody yet even guesses at the mystery surrounding her birth.

Except the Minister himself. Who is not, naturally, her father.

Esther, equally naturally, is very attracted to Felix,

who, to begin with, thinks she is just a pretty butterfly, a would-be fine lady.

Although she is poor she can read, speak and teach French.

To a certain extent, they both misunderstand one another.

The message here is that one should never jump to conclusions

or ever judge people by appearances only . . .

Felix is a Radical, and openly contemptuous of his mother's
  bogus religion –
though not of the Minister and his. At the particular
  moment
when Esther brings her watch to him, he is beginning to thaw
and realise that she isn't as silly as he at first thought she
  might be.
In addition to her parentage, there are other things that
  aren't known.
Neither of them know, for example, that watches and
  intricate machinery
are potent dream-symbols for the female organs.
For a girl to offer her watch to a man means something –
it's an offer of her complete sexual system for him to tinker
  with.
Felix is as innocent as she is. He's never heard of the
  acronym CUVA,
which signifies the female genitals as they are, from North to
  South:
Clitoris, Urethra, Vagina, Anus.
They don't think of such things. But in her unconscious
  Esther
knows what she is doing – if she doesn't, why does she blush?

So she breaks down and cries, and clasps her little gloved
  hands.
Very soon she feels the big hand of Felix
covering them both and pressing them firmly . . .

Nobody should think that I'm mocking George Eliot
or Mary Anne Evans or girls of dubious parentage,
as they read this undithyrambic outpouring.
Felix Holt is a jolly good book,
Felix himself is a sympathetic character,
and so is Esther, and so is the Minister . . .

but in 1865 they looked at a different kaleidoscope.

Relicts, as It Were

All ordinary life goes on.
Hilary Bardwell, Monica Jones
have heard the poets bursting out
in very unbardic tones.

They cut themselves while shaving
and shout out, vatically, *Fuck it!*
Such things are common as breakfast,
before they kick the bucket.

Good writers aren't the supermen
for which some groupies take them.
They're blokes with one special talent –
and talent can forsake them –

they're ordinary boring old persons,
with the drawbacks of the old;
they're never angels of genius,
as we were formerly told.

We're left behind to treasure
the golden things they wrote –
which nevertheless can tarnish.
Like Biblical Joseph's coat

bards don't shine bright for ever;
men, women, old bores, old bags.
Old Yeats was right to say the flesh
gets tattered into rags!

They made their marks on paper.
We're left behind, to read.
Don't worry about their bleeding hearts
(anyone's heart can bleed),

for Christ's sake, don't deify them,
just stick to the printed text.
As Joyce wrote, expecting each moment,
always, to be your next!

Being Good

'Ein guter Mensch sein! Ja, wer wär's nicht gern?' – Bertold
Brecht, *Die Dreigroschenoper*

When you're reading *Little Women* by Louisa M. Alcott
you have, imaginatively, to go back to 1868,
when it was written – when Dickens was still alive
and the reaction against what the Twenties called his
    sentimentality
hadn't yet begun (and Wilde was one of the first ones
to call in question the tear-jerking young female deathbeds).
Pickwick Papers, indeed, was one of Alcott's admired books
and in the novel is very specifically mentioned.
Meg, Jo, Beth and Amy start their own Pickwick Club
for home entertainment. The novel's story, roughly,
was later pinched by Nesbit for *The Railway Children*.
E.g. Dad is away (at the Civil War or in prison)
and Mum and the kids, on their own, have to manage . . .

Pilgrim's Progress is invoked, how each has his burden.
It's a very stoical, Protestant sort of story –
though there is charity dispensed to the penurious Irish
(whose lingo is treated, more or less, as serio-comic)
and a pious Catholic French maid has the right stuff in her.
Good people can be rich, like the Laurences,

or good-hearted but worldly and vulgar like the Moffats,
who aspire always to 'good' marriages and elegance.
Unexpected presents are the currency downwards,
presents of food or a neat little piano.
'Cuddle your cats and get over your headache!'
is the sort of thing one girl will say to another.

Wise and loving, there is no one like Marmee.
She inspires the girls to work old Mr Laurence a pair of
    slippers.
Though he lives next door, and is a millionaire, there is no
    ulterior motive.
Likewise his teenage son. Who, to Jo, can talk about cricket.
Cricket! Jo is just one of the boys. (Not a word about
    baseball.)

Yes, Jo is the tomboy. She wears a broad-brimmed old-
    fashioned Leghorn
(sent for a joke by young Laurie) on a waterborne outing –
'. . . it's capital, – so shady, light and big.
It will make fun; and I don't mind being a guy if I'm
    comfortable.'

An English boy cheats at croquet
('The Englishers played well; but the Americans played
    better')
by nudging the ball with his toe. Jo cries 'You pushed it; I
    saw you.'
She restrains herself (as Marmee would wish) from saying
    something terribly rude.
There is a Yankee victory.

At the same picnic there is an object lesson in English
    snobbery.
Miss Kate makes Meg uncomfortable because she doesn't
    know German
and shows how the English despise people poorer than they
    are

35

and (how very truly) how badly they treat governesses and
  tutors.
But Meg is the prettiest of the whole bunch, notwithstanding.

(Don't forget, the Civil War is going on all this time –
Dad is at it, working away as a padre.
He falls dangerously ill and Marmee goes to him.)

And everywhere there is a work ethic, and Jesus is the
  Friend
and they are all Pilgrims, and trying hard to be good.
Even when they go into a wood in the summer
they take their work with them, holiday tasks as it were.

Yes, most importantly, they are all working at being good,
in the hope of making it to the Celestial City –
'just as generous and patient and good as he can be',
  that's the ticket.
And then Beth nurses the Hummels' baby, as it dies of
  scarlet fever,
gets it herself and Dr Bangs zooms in. Marmee's still with
  Dad,
still desperately ill at the War. And so is Beth,
only rousing now and then to mutter 'Water',
with lips so parched they could hardly shape the word.
She gets worse and worse and worse. Marmee is sent for.
Beth turns the corner . . .
Never had the sun risen so beautifully,
and never had the world seemed so lovely,
as it did to the heavy eyes of Meg and Jo,
as they looked out in the early morning,
when their long, sad vigil was done . . .
'Hark!' cried Jo, starting to her feet.
Yes, there was a sound of bells at the door below,
a cry from Hannah, and then Laurie's voice saying,
in a joyful whisper, 'Girls, she's come! She's come!'

What they are all against are fashionable accomplishments
and being carried away by smart clothes, rings and 'pretty
  things'.
Meg plays the piano, Jo writes, Amy models in clay,
and Beth is just adorable.
Dad comes back, to general rejoicing,
and holds a kind of headmasterly End of Term assessment,
telling how they are all making progress in their goodness
(a novel like *American Psycho* is very far in the future).
Meg (17) gets engaged to Laurie's virtuous young tutor.
Jo and Laurie are (so far) just two good fellows together.
But it's a happy, Dickensian, virtue-triumphant ending –
Pickwickian, turkey-eating, euphoric, even a glass or two of
  wine . . .

This was Alcott's own life, transmuted. The realism
must have been a relief from some of that century's romantic
  nonsense.
Do-gooding self-satisfied prigs? No, I think not.

Perhaps we laugh, perhaps we smile in a superior way,
to think that people were once so earnest.
Yet even great poets can feel they'd like to be good.
Most people, you might say, would like to be good –
accepted by society, not hated or avoided . . .
but it should go, as Alcott says, deeper than conformism.

It's a good book, in its own way, though not a great one.

Watching 'Twin Peaks' While There's a War On

So we see the rock line and the waterfall
and the marvellously pretty young girls

lie on their backs with their twin peaks prominent
and the rushing of the waters is like something from vaginas –
this is all, in every way, as the Director intended.
If it's unconscious, it's not very unconscious . . .

In the middle of the episodes a war is struggling
to make itself felt. While Audrey is in bondage
some poor buggers, equally young, are in the war machine –
struggling to get out. By death, surrender, desertion.
The most pathetic, the bereft Iraqi soldiers,
turn themselves in for unlooked-for food and water . . .

Here the top dogs are the ones with the fire-power,
though, like Agent Cooper, they can make mistakes.
They can bomb a bit carelessly. But the wise (or unwise) telly
never distinguishes between a fact and a fantasy.
Vice-President Quayle stands by like a dildo,
hoping perhaps that one day they may use him.

Meanwhile the girls die, the lads die. Laura Palmer
is an image, just as the war dead are also images
(that, in any detail, we are not allowed to see).
Everything in the end, the set says, is television.
If we're moved, or frightened, or even entertained,
this is a trick (or several tricks) of the light.

Pickled

So we're in the Metropolitan Museum of Art,
all wearing our little lapel buttons
as we venture into European Paintings.

Oh, Bicci di Lorenzo (1373–1452),
how you interest and even amuse us
with your panels concerning the life of St Nicholas!

One depicts the Saint revivifying
'Three Youths pickled by an Innkeeper
during a time of famine' – says the citation.

They stand brown and upright in their pickle jars,
naked, and their top halves only are visible.
The Saint is giving them the Word.

Behind him stands the Innkeeper,
looking wicked and a bit cheesed off.
He must lament the loss of that profitable protein.

The Thirties

Ah, did you once see Spender plain,
   And tow-haired awkward Auden?
In days when politics meant Spain?
   And Art Paul Nash and Bawden?

When Christopher was an Issyvoo
   And Eliot primly clerical,
When Joyce and Pound knew a thing or two
   (And Edith Sitwell hysterical)?

When great Virginia was a Woolf
   And Wyndham Lewis a lion,
While C. S. Lewis had Beowulf
   And Betjeman Mount Zion?

Did you see Layard in a chair,
  Sitting there and talking?
Lys with Elizabeth Bergner hair
  And Connolly fatly walking?

And smooth John Lehmann, eagle-tall,
  With the good looks of an eagle,
An editor – one of the best of all?
  (But his sex-life was illegal.)

And Blunt and Burgess and the boys
  Who haunted their vicinity,
The intellectuals with poise
  In Apostolic Trinity?

The young see *something* of a decade
  But they have an underview – just
The Caterpillar has it made.
  The Alices (me and you) just

Don't see much but the mushroom stalk.
  The rulers sit there smoking.
You think we might have done more than talk?
  You must be joking!

Note: To their eternal credit, some of that generation did do more than talk.
John Cornford, for example, was killed in Spain in 1936.

The Latency Period Ends at Eleven

When we were very young,
at about the time that 'Blue' Milne (A.A.)
was writing those poems

(let's say November 1924)
my cousin and I, walking up Oxford Street,

couldn't understand why women
had such short legs and such broad bottoms
and were, generally, so unathletic,

couldn't understand why they teetered on heels
that would have made it hard for them to run on a football
    field,

couldn't understand just what was the point of them.
Though we'd heard of sex and the mystery of marriage,
and, in my case, the Head of my prep school
later enlightened me in a cryptic kind of way
with dark sayings about the penis being a tap
(he wasn't American, he didn't say 'faucet').

What were they doing, what were they there for?
They were different, but why?

Soon the at-first-not-understood stories at public schools
came to our rescue.

Blake in England 1988

The teacups of the bourgeoisie
mean we never can be free.

The knives that terrify the streets
make God's heart miss several beats.

The Devil enters in his log
each badger baited by a dog.

In Hell rejoicing of the rats
is caused by those who ill-treat cats.

The black man sings his undersong;
his Purgatory is white, and long.

The poor who sleep in cardboard boxes
are less at home than urban foxes.

The weapons in the silos moan –
for all these things, we shall atone.

The Fogg Art Museum at Harvard

This is where the old Italian painters with the joke names
hang out –
Defendente Ferrari, Altobello Melone.
Painting pictures is only playing games,
Art brings nothing about –

once Auden in his heyday certainly thought (and said).
They're actors,
the people in pictures are really phoney.
There's one where a wan woman lies in bed.
With a member like a cactus,

erect and bristly, a Devil (*The* Devil?) takes his leave,
exorcised.

'The Miracle Of St Catherine'. Showing peasants
(St Catherine in charge, with nothing up her sleeve)
how wicked sex, surprised,

can be overcome by prayer (and she's praying like mad)?
So perhaps
peasant behaviour *was* steered from these Unpleasants,
(say) a virgin warned off a stinking cad
and Pleasure's tickling traps?

Sex Education

Round about the time when Hitler
got to be Chancellor of Germany,
in 1933 or so, when she was 11,
my wife began that monstrous menstruation
that so disgusted all the medieval monks . . .

She was a boarder in a convent school,
nobody told her a thing about what was coming.

At first she thought she was bleeding to death.
She got into a loo and stuffed her knickers with paper –
it was that shiny-stiff paper called Bronco,
not absorbent like the modern tender tissues.

Almost at once, as she walked with a friend,
she began to creak and squeak as she walked.
'What's that funny noise?' said the friend.

You could say, if you were philosophical,
it was the noise of obscurantism, throughout history,
or the hardly-heard complaint of a victim.

The Joy of the Sadists

(Found Poem: *Guardian*, *London*, *11th May 1990*)

Flames shot from a man's shaven skull
six inches into the air
when the electrocution of a
convicted murderer in Florida last week
went badly wrong,
state prison officials have confirmed.

A synthetic sponge was substituted by mistake
for the natural sponge
which is usually used to ensure
good conductivity between the skullcap electrode
and the shaven head
of the condemned man.

Witnesses watched flames, smoke and sparks
shooting from the head of Jessie Tafero,
as the prison authorities carried out the sentence and,
regardless of the victim's plight,
administered three successive
2,000-volt blasts of electricity.

'No execution is pleasant to watch,
but this was abnormal,'
Bob McMaster, a witness who works
for the Florida Corrections Department,
said yesterday . . .

'I guess it goes to show
you have to use natural products,'
Mr McMaster commented.

Packages

In the American Phase there was a deep Nannification.
Auden's language became increasingly childish.
Isn't there a poem addressed to a woman
in which he says 'You and I have bottoms of different
    shapes'?
Or words to that effect . . .

In fact, every poet is a product. We have an expectation.
One is fierce, one is cissy, one is mildish.
It's certain we had expectations of Auden.
We don't like poets who fool about. No one escapes.
We all, like England, expect.

One lives by gay rhetoric, one by entropy with animals,
one is a 'war poet', one has 'secret narrative' –
whatever it is, we expect it; and any sudden
change is never thought of as a change for the better.
We don't like it much.

We don't want the missionaries to turn into cannibals.
If he's a tonic, he must stay restorative;
the hermetic bard must always be hidden.
It's bad form, like suddenly not using a French letter,
to come out of the hutch

(or out of the sophisticated hat of the evening-dressed
    conjuror)
a completely different and altered rabbit
from the one that went in. We harden
our attitudes, they set firm as amateur toffee.
Almost, slogans

define the poets – 'Not waving but drowning', etcetera –
a despair in four words. Like hypochondriacs of habit,
we know that 'Phyllosan Fortifies the Over-Forties'. Garden
gnomes stand around like idols. We drink tea or coffee
and watch our Wogans . . .

knowing that each poet is a very separate package
and comes in one form, always, and standard.
It's nice for the poets, too, not to stand like a lemon
unrecognised. Their worth is known, you might consider,
some are light, some heavy,

some masculine, some feminine, they have tenure, socage
or status (you might say) for their services rendered.
They're brand names, idiosyncratic and human,
they're not sold as a job lot to the highest bidder
like slaves, in a bevy.

'Not Once or Twice in Our Rough Island Story'

My youth was blighted by
a dirty great war.
From it some generals and politicians
had some glory –
but for the rest of us
it was a long and gory
old bore!

Think of poor young soldiers
all shitting themselves
in those final instinctual battlefield
natural terrors!

Thousands of books now lie
(top brass – their mighty errors)
on shelves . . .

Explained, debated, analysed,
apologised for!
This is the second load that we carry;
white heat of battle
gives way to all this gossipy
exculpatory tittle-tattle
of War.

A Little Larkinish Lyric

We're all of us,
lewd and lowly, high and hymnlike holy,
moving, quickly or slowly,
into the category of those who don't know
what day it is.
Yes, that's the way it is.

We're all of us,
loony left or raving right, and deft or
clumsy, cared for, bereft or
much of a muchness, average, so-so,
resigned, fretful,
getting more forgetful . . .

What all of us
forget simply, beauties and the pimply,
as we go stiffly or limply
into oblivion, that long night of snow,
is how bad it was
and (luckily) how sad it was.

In Praise of Alan Brownjohn

There's a smile on the face of the tiger –
but the tiger is always around.
You won't track him down with a Geiger,
he will creep up without any sound
and be on you. A leap and a bound!

Our life, like the tiger, has beauty –
but it's terrible too. (Just read Blake.)
Though we live with a strong sense of duty,
don't think we'll survive. No mistake,
it is not just one sweet piece of cake!

And the bards worth the price of admission
are the ones who know this, such as you.
Our reality's nuclear fission
and those dreams of delight aren't quite true.
Those who know this, are first of the few.

Cats and Bags
(The Cruelty of the Emperor)

'The cruelty of the emperor [Theodore Lascaris II] was
exasperated by the pangs of sickness, the approach of a
premature end, and the suspicion of poison and magic . . .
A matron of the family of the Palaeologi had provoked his
anger by refusing to bestow her beauteous daughter on the
vile plebeian who was recommended by his caprice. Without

regard to her birth or age, her body, as high as the neck, was inclosed in a sack with several cats, who were pricked with pins to irritate their fury against their unfortunate fellow-captive.' – Gibbon, *The Decline and Fall of the Roman Empire*, Chapter LXII.

What's funny? There's always something cruel in what's
     funny.
William Plomer would have enjoyed this story.
'An old bag in a bag' – you can imagine the poem – how
     hilarious!
Hard-hearted verse, slightly obscene; as they once said,
     'curious',
like the bombed horse-haunch landing smack on a vegetarian
     table –
a warning to cranks, a kind of moral cautionary fable.

But I think this whole thing has a different kind of
     resonance,
it's uneasy, like giving up standard rhyme for assonance.
To begin with, it's cruelty to cats – 'a part to tear a cat in'
remember, once meant exactly that, you can put that in
your *History of Cruelty*; and on Bonfire Night, disgusting
it now seems, they burned cats, there was cat-
     combustion . . .

And, if you consider the state of mind and health of the
     Emperor,
he wasn't exactly happy, he wasn't like Beecham or
     Klemperer
romping away with Mozart or Beethoven. He was extremely
     sick.
In those days if a King didn't like you, he could cut off your
     prick.
He *could* have been nastier to her. Use your imagination.
They used to do terrible things to unpopular statesmen.

So I think what I think is that nobody did well out of it,
life-enhancing it wasn't, there can be no doubt of it.
Perhaps the vile plebeian profited most from the deal –
unless the beauteous daughter liked rough trade. So I feel
the matron was morally best, the cats neutral, there's no
    deep
moral. Except that an Emperor can often be a bit of a creep.

Fear of Living/Fear of Dying

Engines falling off the Boeings!
What a lot of frightening goings-on!
Danger in the air – and, grounded,
Murders! We are quite surrounded!
We're not *safe* – it's all a mighty con!

Who, with breakfast in his tummy,
Knows he won't meet with some rummy do?
Be quite *dead* before his dinner?
Never get from Poole to Pinner?
Moving on – but what's he moving *to*?

Death comes newer than the newest,
Hawklike power-dives from the bluest skies!
Drink the wine and eat the wafer,
Cross your fingers, you're not safer –
Death can be a nasty big surprise!

The Quiet Ones

Stevie was never in Pop
she was in Palmer's Green
her secludedness didn't stop
how can I say what I mean?
She didn't socialise
she didn't play fast and loose
really I suppose what I mean
is she was a sort-of
sort-of recluse.

Larkin lay hidden in Hull
with the grim head-scarved wives
he liked it backward and dull
with the unflamboyant lives.
There's a lot to be said for a bard
who doesn't spread it around
that's what I'm saying now
it's best to be foxlike and go
go to ground.

Emily Dickinson too
buried herself and took root
those who saw her were few
there was no trumpeting toot
her talent lay quiet behind drapes
the others didn't know
though in her lifetime Bohemians
often behaved like Poe
like a so-and-so.

Hopkins was lost and unknown
till Bridges unsleeved that ace
no agents flocked to the phone.
TV is the Great Good Place

a good many people think –
but you don't really need a repeat
learn it young and you'll know it all
from even the most far-back
back seat!

22 West Cromwell Road

(Cabaret Song)

In front of the house
there's a barricading hoarding
(and the windows are practically none) –
it's a piece of anti-vandal tatty-looking boarding;
and the roof that kept out
the rain and the sun,
its time is almost done.

Underneath that roof
was the starting of our marriage,
it was thirty-three years ago now –
marriage is a something that sophisticates disparage,
and no one would claim that
at all times, everyhow,
it should be a sacred cow . . .

but it was in that flat
(or a duplex you could call it)
that two kids passed their immature days,
so I'm sighing for that house and the fate that will befall it –
we were happy in the
small family ways;
it very seldom pays

to look back at the past
or get songlike sentimental

but I know that the ball-and-chain bash
won't much care for *us* or be sorrowful and gentle –
because a house is only,
and always only, CASH
and a kind of valued trash.

22 May 1989

Note: The tune on which this is (very roughly) based is Kurt Weill's 'I Am a
Stranger Here Myself', from *One Touch of Venus*, his Broadway show of 1943.
The gentle/sentimental rhyme comes from Noel Coward ('Try to Learn to
Love').

Roy Fuller

He's a very fine poet who po-
tentially could have two po-
ems or more in any anthology or inventory
of the best English poems of this century.

Classical and restrained, no passions carry him away, a low pass-
ion for Dylan Thomas rhetoric he never had,
but there's feeling, as much as the great ones ever had . . .

We all trust him, you see, 'sensible' is the word; but agree sens-
itivity is there too in his writing personality,
you can't deny that he can heighten reality.

All those with brains have noticed
that what's absent is the egotist-
ical sublime. Instead, he's analytical,
and (in the best sense of the word) he's political.

Sgt. Paul

Go up to a black sheep and tap him on the shoulder:
                    Why not try Jesus?
There's something odd about those weaker vessels.
                    They're full of girlpee.
And so much in the Pentagon is beyond understanding.
                    So why were we chosen?

We are only worms. The logistics of conversion
                    Can stall a computer.
He sent us out to do our best with Asia,
                    SNAFU as usual.
A small band of experts with love and equipment.
                    Beyond the grave: Heaven.

And we succeed more, the more we can put there,
                    Making them angels.
Giving them another life. For we can redeem them
                    In the Hereafter.
We argue that paddy fields are grossly material,
                    Not things of the spirit.

So for their own good we disintegrate the body,
                    Knowing that the Harvest
Shall be, on that Last Day, unbelievably smashing.
                    They will be blooming
Over that dry land like big flowers and rice-shoots.
                    To meagre us – credit.

So we knock off the safety catch. Metal is persuasive.
                    In the True Way advisers
Can show how in mercy the guns bless a hillside,
                    And how the blasphemers
Are full of soft liberal talk and misunderstand us,
                    Fat yellowbellies.

He trained us for this. We do our poor best but
                    ╱Fall short of the perfect.
Our Love is terrifying, and terrifyingly stupid
                         To the snobs and highbrows.
We are beyond the understanding of the brainy.
                         God Rose – man trellis!

Sex Being Remarkable

If Bondage Lesbians are tying up Lesbians,
if SM Gays hammer nails through penises
(sex being remarkable),

if the summer's the time for the Murder of Minors,
if the Respectables dream of all kinkiness
(sex being remarkable),

if the Secret Police give jobs to the torturers,
if women are stuffed with harmful alternatives
(sex being remarkable),

if the Mutilators are politically acceptable,
if the Best Massacres are even now occurring
(sex being remarkable),

it's a wonder any practice can be thought of as normative
and the beds of Britain can feel snug and average –
sex being so remarkable!

Byron, Shelley and their Circle

Look at it from any angle,
it's still a terrible tangle –
if Shelley saw anything young and female
he would live with it or marry it . . .
and this certainly led to the suicide of Harriet.

And, like a corsair, Byron
was keen to open fire on
any bright frigate that crossed his bowsprit –
gipsy, gondolier's wife, Contessa, nigra or negra
or Clare Clairmont, the mother of Allegra.

With side effects – Hogg, Trelawny –
happy when the port was tawny
(like the witty Peacock), while talented Mary
wrote *Frankenstein*, and the philosophic Godwin . . .
God? Never let *that* old sod win!

So, from where I'm sitting,
it looks like beginner's knitting –
poor Fanny killed herself with laudanum.
Leigh Hunt was no Barrett of the Street called Wimpole –
though Dickens made him a sponger (Harold Skimpole).

They meant well, they weren't tarty
at the Villa Diodati
or at Marlow – the working class did worse,
they just starved and were hanged for High Treason –
but pure happiness didn't follow the pursuit of Pure Reason.

Mac U Seka-Ru

(A Glosa Elegy for George MacBeth)

O George, homo u pani-bo-pe in u pani-bo,
tu pa vive hedo in poesi! Stili, grafo-mo!
Regi-an de prosa plus-co, tu pa skribe bibli
ke ko verba ko zelo abili toxi
panto-pe, an e fe! Plu anua retro
mi pa encontra tu. Nu panto-lo
klu in plu kuko-ka, mu ski, de MacBeth, plus ergo!

U karakteri de fascina! Mo kilo kron ma boni
de multi plu poeta, idio, mega preci!

English Translation

Mac The Knife

O George, like a baker in a baker's shop,
you lived happily in poetry! Pen, desk!
King of prose too, you wrote books
that with word and vitality could enchant
everybody, man and woman! Some years ago
I met you. Now everywhere,
even in kitchens, they know the works of MacBeth!

A character of charm! A thousand times better
than many poets, unique, truly precious!

Part Two: 'Frivolous'

Snow White (1989)

She's a widow-maker
and a credit-taker,
everything good's due to *her* –
it's not accident,
she's Heaven-sent,
she can only sit and purr

as the cream grows richer
and the culture kitscher –
and there's no dissenting voice
as the topcats scoff it
and the god called Profit
is the South East English Choice

and the Press grows hottish
as the traitor Scottish
beg to differ a bit;
while the BBC too
she must certainly see to
with her Instant Pressure Kit!

There is homeless weeping
but her Good Housekeeping
will make us happy and strong
and the Future fissile
through each new missile –
you don't get those for a song.

The Falklands Factor
or a dodgy reactor,
she takes them all in her stride,
nothing loth, nothing lother –
the Contras, Piet Botha!
She's not just there for the ride.

Queen of every chat show,
the Crystal Cat Show
never ever produced such a cat,
worshipped by Wogan,
her personal slogan:
I'm right, never wrong! And that's that!

American Presidents (Calypso Style)

When de New President go to de toilet he fin'
dat de Ol' President done left a load o' shit behin' –

it do sticky his fingers and with all his might
he curse de Ol' President for all dis shite!

He tink it a most low an' disgustin' caper,
and to clear it up he's gonna need loads o' paper!

Statements an' affidavits an' transcripts an' trials –
de paper dat's needed is miles and miles and miles!

He'd like to say 'What da muddaskunt you done, man?
You cause more trouble dan is right for one man!'

But de Ol' President, he's away for life
in a marble mansion wi' his wondrous wife!

He's asleep wi' a knowing little grin showin' on he face –
he won't never go back to dat White House place!

You won't get at him all de winter through,
he's a hibernatin' hedgehog – he don' heed *you!*

He don' mind if dem teevee preachers
has private lives wi' exceptional features!

He don' need no upper, he don' need no downer,
he jes' goes on sleepin' an' his hair gets browner!

What does he care if de world go wrong?
He's sleepin', a-singin' dat Ol' President Song!

New President, he worry sick, he where de volcano bubble.
Ol' President, he sleep tight – 'cos he ain't got no trouble!

January 1990

Final Test v. West Indies, 12th August 1991 (McGonagallesque Victory Ode)

What a team to beat!
As talented as a centipede with two hundred feet!
('What a city to sack!' was once said, of London, by
    Blucher.)

Test cricket is like a sort of very complicated out-door
    snooker,
it depends on timing and tactics and luck and resources –
you've got to know when to go for it and when to hold your
    horses . . .

Think first of their four fiery fast bowlers,
grinding away at the batsmen like inexorable molars,

able to make a good-length ball quite steeply climb
on that true, hard Oval wicket, time after time . . .

Think of Walsh, who makes funny faces
and has big round eyes like a lemur's,
a force to be reckoned with in the land of the seamers;
and even more of Ambrose (first name Curtly)
who from his great height bangs in the short ball very
   expertly;
and think of Patterson, if you are able,
as tall as they, and who looks like a black Clark Gable . . .
but, most of all, nobody could remain impartial
confronted by the genius and cunning of the veteran
   Marshall,
still listed as the World No. 1.

All very hard to score off. And when they've done,
and you've been defending away like a trooper,
you still have to deal with the accurate guile of a Hooper,
an outstanding spinner, adept at flighting
his slow temptations, and over-exciting
the best batsmen at their stolidest . . .

Then look at their batting, one of the solidest
line-ups in the world! What remains,
in the way of praise, to be said about Haynes?
And what about Richardson? Indeed, what?
There simply isn't a batsmanly virtue that he hasn't got!
Footwork, judgement, the lot . . . driving, glancing,
   steering . . .

and ditto for Viv Richards, though he's more buccaneering,
more of a stroke-proud dandy,
eating up bad bowling as a kid eats candy!

Go through the order, it's a marvellous card.
Hooper again, and Dujon and Marshall always die hard!

A free-scoring lot, and a challenge for the bard!

So how was it done? Well, mostly by Gooch . . .
He showed the other batsmen the way. Not given to smooch
(or to hooch) he insisted on fitness,
good fielding, catches held . . . and the result bears witness!

We feel sad for Jack Russell, that little barking terrier . . .
it's a matter of runs, you might say, the more the merrier,
and Alec Stewart could make them. And his keeping was
  good.
Even to the wayward pace of Lawrence. It's always been
  understood
that a batsman/wicketkeeper is superior to just a pure
  keeper –
he's a sleeping partner, as it were, an inactive spy, a
  'sleeper'.

Robin Smith comes next to Gooch, extreme aggression
being able to cheer us up in a time of recession . . .
and Ramprakash, and don't forget the absent Pringle
(the occasional boundary, the fairly frequent single),
whose bowling was so consistently restrictive
on those batsmen whose stroke-making was addictive . . .

But De Freitas deserves the biggest hand of all.
He was always troublesome to them, ball after ball.
Lawrence too, of course, his big enthusiastic mate,
he really came up with the goods when he bowled straight.
Lewis too, with bat and ball, deserves our praise.
He did us proud (that seems the right phrase).

And in this last victorious match
you can't ignore Botham – bowl, bat, catch,
he did a full Nelson ('England expects . . .').
He was one of the big guns.
And, naturally enough, he scored the winning runs.

Of course no team ever selects
itself. But Tufnell was a very inspired choice,
and 6 for 25! With no dissenting voice
we must give him the credit for the spell that won the
game . . .

What we must hope for in the World Cup is more of the
same!

Native Girls and British Sailors

We native girls love the British sailors,
we love their big red noses,
we love their big red cocks –
and darning their socks!

Every girl wants a British sailor,
their big red hands are lovely,
they're feeling up our skirts –
we're washing their shirts!

We can't do without a British sailor,
we love their rum and salt-beef;
although they're not good-looking,
we do all their cooking!

We native girls love the British sailors,
we love their drunken singing,
we sing their favourite shanties
(we're not wearing panties)!

We really love their reeling hornpipes,
the randy boozy dancing –
we love their big red feet.
We think they're so sweet!

We native girls all shack up with sailors,
we love their rum love-making,
those Billies, Bobs and Sids –
and having their kids!

Georgetown, Guyana, 7 November 1989

University Nights!

(After 57 years)

Oh, those misty Cambridge evenings,
where the cold fog sways and swirls!
Of what were all the thinkers thinking?
        Answer: girls!

Dons ate silvered buttered crumpets,
rehearsing professional ploys,
fine minds honed to one clear concept
        only: boys!

Drinking rum and Coca-Cola,
gin and tonic, thoughtful Yanks
for traditional snorts and snifters
        gave much thanks!

Dons High-Tory-disputatious!
(There are still some of that sort.)
In the storm of modern living,
           seeking port!

King's Parade, the Backs – idyllic!
As the rowing men's muscles flex,
there's no change. Then. Now. Two targets:
           drink (drugs), sex!

From 'The Songs and Sonnets of Ruperta Bear'

Haiku: Mortality

Like flies in the days
of fly-papers we all come
to a sticky end.

An Unsavoury Nursery Rhyme

The Queen is in the parlour,
slowly masturbating;
and in the King's stuprarium
the Ladies line up, waiting!

Cricket Threnody: On Allan Lamb's Claudication

O ovine limb, O lamblike leg!
O sadness of a leg of Lamb!
Hear me, O Gods, we humbly beg,
And lend ear to our dithyramb
In honour of that legless Lamb
And heal our limping choriamb,
Peg-leg that takes us down a peg!

25 July 1988

D. H. Lawrence

The sperms were tumbling like waterfalls,
pistils were pissing, there were standing stamens,
everything was overflowing in torrents –
       and *Flowers are so sexy!* said D. H. Lawrence.

Like in shooting galleries, bobbling balls –
as vestal virgins, shamans, flamens,
when Lorenzo went so batty in Florence.
       Lilies aren't silly, said D. H. Lawrence.

It was quite like a song from the music halls,
and the Venus Girls all screamed big Amens,
and Decency Leagues expressed abhorrence . . .
       but *The Gods are dark*, said D. H. Lawrence.

Discover the True Stories of a Royal Home

(Advertisement on the London Underground)

At Hampton Court, fat Henry's Royal Palace,
Discover the true stories of a Royal Home!
He was no niggard with his active phallus
At Hampton Court, fat Henry's Royal Palace –
Not different much from oil-rich lust in Dallas
Or what the Popes were into, in old sexy Rome!
At Hampton Court, fat Henry's Royal Palace,
Discover the true stories of a Royal Home!

T. S. Eliot and the Demotic

You don't need to have read Matthew Arnold, Sophocles and
The Golden Bough
to know that T. S. Eliot never said 'Ta-ta for now!'
nor do you need to read the old philosophers and such
to know that he didn't, either, say 'Ta very much!'

Sea Song

A big boy kneels at the edge of the sea,
A big balloon brandy there by his knee . . .
Whisper who dares! Credibility fails.
Kingsley Amis is singing to whales!

Fartarsing About in the Army, AD 1071–1072

(The Decline and Fall of the Roman Empire, Chapter LVI)

'Of odd particulars,' Gibbon
'learned from Malaterra . . .
that the bite of the tarantula
provokes a windy disposition,
*quae per anum inhoneste crepitando
emergit*; a symptom most ridiculously felt
by the whole Norman army
in their camp near Palermo.'

Life in AD 1291

Adenalf of Anagnia*
was the slave of algolagnia.
When reality failed
he had fantasies of being impaled.

---

* Falsely considered to have been the author of *De Excidio urbis Acconis*, one
  of the important sources regarding the Siege of Acre.

Stung by a West Indian Wasp

It wasn't an ant or a bee –
I was stung by a black Follow Me!
Yes, it jolly well did!
As of now I'm a kid
That can't speak, smell, and hardly can see!

Note: The Follow Mes are big black wasps (but not as big as the Marabuntas, which can be as large as people's fingers). They live in Guyana, where they are so called because they actually do pursue their victims.

Mrs C. B. Fry

I am truly the first of the Gorgons
and my gaze turns the lads into stone,
I'm more magic than fairies called Morgans
and the Navy shakes when I intone:
THEY ARE USING THEIR RACIAL ORGANS
FOR PURPOSES OF THEIR OWN!

The Limitations of Rugby League Players

They know about Rugby League,
they know about pussy;
but they don't know anything about
Debussy.

Porphyria's Lover

You know that poem by Browning
where this lunatic sits quietly by this girl,
whom he's strangled with her own long blonde hair?
There would have been struggles and convulsions
and an absolute storm of shit and piss –
but Browning doesn't seem to know (or care)
about this!

Commentary

The best thing about cricket on the radio
is that you can shout at Trueman
at the top of your voice:
'You moombling, boombling, big-'eaded North Coontry twit!'
and he won't come round and thump you!

A Little Loyal Ode to the Queen Mother on her 90th Birthday

Elizabeth Bowes-Lyon! It is fit that we
should drink to you in a very large G and T!
Mainly because you've been around so long
but also because you thought *The Waste Land* by T. S. Eliot
was called *The Desert Song!*

The Triumph and Injury of Ian Botham, 23rd/24th May 1991

When the great Bottybogs
puts on his cricket togs
even the most hardened clog-dancer forgets his clogs!
(This is the time of the waking-up of hedgehogs.)
After the winter fogs
everyone wants Bottybogs,
the devoted woman dog-handler neglects her dogs –
he is the ratchet and we are the cogs!

You could say Athertigger
is, in a way, bigger –
he's certainly taller, and a very batsmanlike figure
(at whom nobody could possibly snigger),
sails on like an outrigger –
but it's gin in a jigger
that Botty is like, in his full cricketing vigour!
The bane of the Windy and the outspoken Digger!

So when he takes 4 for 45
we all feel more alive –
his is the perfection towards which we strive,
his is the finest cut and the hardest drive,
he is the biggest bee in the hive,
he makes the lost cause thrive,
those odds of 500 to 1 very quickly dive –
when *he* gets to the crease all our hopes revive!

Injury to him injures us,
like being run over by a bus,
and causes a tremendous lot of fuss –
a hamstring can very easily nonplus
even great cricketers, and thus

each old boy who wears a truss
explodes in woe like a blunderbuss –
the young lads too, the goody-goody and the awkward cuss!

May 1991

Note: There have been later and greater triumphs since this poem was written. The match referred to was a one-day international, England v. West Indies (which England narrowly won, largely because of Botham's bowling and Atherton's batting). Botham injured a hamstring in going for a run. The childish versions of Botham's and Atherton's names are inspired by the nursery end of the cricket-lovers' spectrum. Compare the football fans who call Gascoigne 'Gazza'.

The Thomas Hardy Section

1. T.R.O.T.N.*

Diggory Venn and Eustacia Vye
were as Hardyesque as pie in the sky –
if German philosophers ambled by,
asking 'Ven?' and asking 'Vy?'
(or even asking Venn and Vye),
Hardy would hardly deign to reply.
Hardy knew, from start to finish,
the age-old Ironies don't diminish!

* *The Return of the Native*

2. Found Poem

(*from* The Woodlanders)

Fitzpiers left the cot,
and the stroke of his feet was soon immersed
in the silence that pervaded the spot.

3. Marty South's Letter to Edred Fitzpiers

(The Woodlanders, *end of Chapter XXXIV*)

Deer Mister Fitzpiers

A'm writen to thee now to tell thee
what may lie heavy on thy belly!

Yon hiair that Barber Percomb took
that wer *my* hiair, by t' Holy Book,
a zold it to'm, – an' all to deck
proud Mistress Charmond's hiead an' neck!

Zo what thou stroak'st in't hers but mine,
zo pirty, vrom a maid divine
it might a' come! A girt injustice
'tis now to me, vor wheer thy lust is
theer might a' been some love o' *me!*

Zigned: Marty South, o' low degree.

4. *The Allotment of Sex in* The Woodlanders

Mrs Charmond has an awful lot.
So does Suke Damson (she's right on the spot)
and when she finally marries Timothy Tangs
he too has a few bangs.
Edred Fitzpiers, like Mrs C, is another big sexpot,
he rogers Grace Melbury as often as not
(after he's married her, naturally and of course);
he rides about lecherously on a horse
and has a long affair with Felice (Mrs Charmond),
who has Italian pre-Raphaelite eyes shaped like an almond.

But as for poor little Marty South,
she has every reason to feel down in the mouth.
Just like noble Giles Winterborne (who isn't a toff)
she never seems able to have it away, or off.
No one makes an offer to seduce or deprave.
All she can do is put flowers on his grave!

5. *The Thomas Hardy Blues*

Bring me all the accoutrements of a furze-cutter,
the billhook, the leggings, and the gloves!
I want to be a genuine Egdon Heath nutter,

right in the middle of the aristocrats,
the decayed aristocrats, the prosperous farmers and the
    tenants,
and all their frustrated loves . . .

I want, if I can't be a furze-cutter, to be a reddleman,
permanently stained by the sheep-marking vermilion –
I'm not clever, I don't ever want honour and glory, I don't
   want a medal, man;

I don't want to be a diamond merchant
or a rich dairyman, hot among the milkmaids,
I don't want to own Wessex or make a billion . . .

I want to be a quiet observer of all their cock-ups,
how it's always the innocent people like Tess
who end up most frequently in their lock-ups,

and how there are always coincidences and
   misunderstandings,
mistaken trysts, lovers in the wrong places at the right time,
more than any sensible person could ever imagine or guess!

Two Advertising Triolets

Grape-Nuts

'GRAPE-NUTS were created back in 1898 in Battle Creek,
Michigan, by Charles W. Post, who also thought up the
rather unusual name' – *Grape-Nuts packet*

O Childhood breakfast joy, the work of Post,
who also made those works of art, Post-Toasties!
The crunchy cereal that we loved the most,
O childhood breakfast joy, the work of Post,

near your centenary now, great Corn-God ghost!
Homely but elegant like a perfect hostess,
O childhood breakfast joy, the work of Post –
who also made those works of art, Post-Toasties!

Watney's Red Barrel

That most revolting beer, the foul Red Barrel,
was foisted on us by the brewers, Watney's,
on each beer-drinking Dave and Dan and Darrell.
That most revolting beer, the foul Red Barrel,
as sweet and sentimental as 'A Christmas Carol',
widely promoted, Tannochbrae to Totnes,
that most revolting beer, the foul Red Barrel,
was foisted on us by the brewers, Watney's.

Two Little Sado-Masochistic Fantasies

Fantasy One

 HE: I want to rush in and tie you up and fuck you!
SHE: Oh, please don't rush in and tie me up and fuck me!

(He rushes in and ties her up and fucks her)

Fantasy Two

SHE: I want to rush in and tie you up and fuck you!
 HE: Oh, please don't rush in and tie me up and fuck me!

(She rushes in and ties him up and fucks him)

What the Salesman Said

If you live with them, you've got to listen to them.
You can't just turn away or look right through them,
or hide yourself in a corner, or stand on your head.
If you live with them, you've got to listen to them –
    and that is what the salesman said!

If you live with them, you've got to listen to them,
you can't say *Who are you?* or *Pardon?* as though you never
    knew them –
they're not a one-night stand, just good in bed.
If you live with them, you've got to listen to them,
    and that is what the salesman said!

If you live with them, you've got to listen to them,
you can't have them for libel, you can't sue them,
they can say what they like, until they're dead!
If you live with them, you've got to listen to them –
    and that is what the salesman,
    jokingly, fun-pokingly,
    that is what the salesman said!

– The Upstairs Bar, Euston Station, 16 April 1991

Choirboy Chorale (Kirchstetten)

Wer will den dicke Wystan küssen?
Niemand will! Aber wir müssen!
    Wie der Klavierspieler Richter,
    Auden ist ein grosser Dichter!

Wichtig ist er! In den Talen
Berühmt! Internationalen,
    Alle Kritiken harmonieren –
    Lobenswert ist er mit Tieren!

Alle Schöpfung lobt die Lieder,
Ober, unter, über, nieder –
    Zusammenbeissen wir die Zähne!
    Vorwärts geh'n die kleine Hähne!

Translation:
Who will kiss the fat Wystan? Nobody wants to! But we must!
Like the pianist Richter*, Auden is a great poet!
He is important! In the valleys famous! International,
all the Critics sing in harmony: Praiseworthy is he, with the Animals!
All Creation praises the Songs, over, under, above, below –
Let us clench our teeth! Forwards with the little cocks!

* Sviatoslav Richter

Schlitz Malt Liquor

(i.m. Hugh Chisholm)

I take back to my New York hotel
an enormous sandwich, filled with everything.
To drink, I choose a can of Schlitz.
I've never had it before; I choose it solely

because in 1935 or 1936 an American,
in Cambridge, England, told me
a simple American joke:

Girls shouldn't drink beer on the beach –
because if they do, they'll get sand in their Schlitz.

The same man told me the very first
dirty joke that he ever heard. The definition
of a French Breakfast: a roll in bed with honey.

New York, 30 April 1990

To Seamus in Grateful Appreciation of Bed and Breakfast

Seamus, your Irish Breakfast Tea
was just the very tea for me –
it was terrific!
Likewise those Trappist-packed Preserves
were just the things to calm my nerves.
To be specific,

I didn't even venture out
(with my arthritis and my gout)
into a diner.
I breakfasted chez-vous, aloof
under an academic roof –
what could be finer?

My thanks too for the bed, the same
that held my unathletic frame –
ten thousand smackers
would not be much too high a price!
Great! Like the slim and very nice
salt-reduced crackers!

I'm not so perfect, smooth as lawns,
or any dog that rolls and fawns
(most often spaniels).
I did a Dylan Thomas too,
I had three fingers (this is true)
of your Jack Daniels!

For this, forgiveness! If you stray
to London on your Britward way,
a litman's labour,
call us, we're in the book! Disdain
for once the wiles of suave Craig Raine,
and neglect Faber!

Harvard, April 1990

The Sad Sale of a Hospitable House

So many times those stairs
have been happily stumbled up!
At so many drunken affairs
thick speech garbled and mumbled – up
comes the come-uppance at last:
those parties are things of the past!

Goodbye to the wavering tread
and the wit that was often woozy
with the tales of the bottle and bed;
and the beautiful, serious, boozy
Other World goes; with the laughter
that shall not be found here hereafter!

'Fair women and brave men'
but not just the beauty or glory,
humour was healing too then
and Life was a shaggy dog story,
escapist and good for us all
as any old Waterloo Ball!

For Stephen Spender's 81st Birthday

Far nearer sixty years than fifty
since we met at Grigson's party!
Time, of such good meetings thrifty,
mixes arty, tarty, smarty
in its quick kaleidoscope –
friendship's more than we can hope!

All the same, when moons are blueing,
sometimes luck can hit the spot
and good be good and past undoing –
and fortunate – rather than not.
In our muddled world of men,
I believe that happened then!

September 1990

The Tart of the Lower Sixth

What washing of willies!
What spurting of sperm!
Does anyone
Have so much fun
As me – by the end of the term!

What coaxing of condoms!
What rides to a fall!
The Head's fat wife
Would give her life
To have such a beautiful ball!

What prodding by prefects!
What twining of necks!
A *roman noir!*
The whole of the choir
Sings of me and of my oral sex!

I masturbate masters,
The Head's on my list,
I'm proud to say –
Today's his day,
It's his turn to be French-kissed!

Repining, repenting?
I don't shed a tear!
Because I know
I'll be a real pro
By the end of my schoolgirl career!

The Novels of Beryl Bainbridge

If you're a man in a book by Beryl,
believe me, you're in very great peril!
Unsure of purpose, weak and wobbly,
or stern and strong, small bum, knees knobbly,

Accidental-On-Purpose Death
before the end will stop your breath!
You'll find it's a girl who's the great Prime Mover
when your Fate sucks you in like a ghastly Hoover.

Wolves are around in girl-sheep apparel
(just *one* girl once ended up in a barrel).
Truth is no object. Stick out no necks –
and keep away from that opposite sex!

Browning in Cambridge* (1935)

There are dons in Downing, old dons in high-class Corpus,
    Evelyn Hope,
stinking like the poo of a weary half-dead porpoise –
    as I lope
down the King's Parade straight, to a teashop called
                        Fitzbillies
    where I buy
cake; but all the scholars are obsessed quite by their willies –
    so am I!

It's the Greek and all that Latin grammar that fatigues me,
    Evelyn mine,

though yours only is the physiology intrigues me –
    I'm a swine
like the ones in Homer, fornicators fixed by Circe
    in that shape,
not averse to pointing perpendicular Percy
    in a rape!

Richards is th' Athenian that the young men follow.
    English Schools
consider all Victorian verse is very hollow.
    Only fools
now like men like Landor; it's alas that I am failing!
    I can't cope!
So please lap my Lapsang Souchong – while your bosom I am
                              Braille-ing,
    Evelyn Hope!

*'Ewart does his Browning' – Glyn Maxwell, *TLS*, 3 November 1989

Prep School Revelations

At a certain Prep School in England
it was suspected that Miss Ellis was in love with Mr Knight –
we didn't know this directly
but from out-of-school intelligence.
Someone was a cousin of somebody
and somebody (was it Bing?) told us he'd seen
a photo of them both lying on towels on a beach . . .

They all said he had played rugger for Blackheath.

Hearsay was the close companion of our guesswork,
though sometimes actuality broke into our romancing
as when Mr Jones stood up in the dining room one morning
and said to Miss Awdry:
'Now I'm going into the town to get a *proper* breakfast!'

Miss Ellis taught the youngest class.
There was one boy who was always wetting himself.
She made him come out in front of her and turn round,
to see the wet patch on his trousers.
We thought this was odd. It wasn't the *back* of his trousers
that would get wet first.
Perhaps this, in some way, was modesty on her part.

But she wasn't altogether modest.
One day in the summer, she had a class in the playing field.
She sat with her knees drawn up. We could see her knickers,
white cotton stretched over the mount of Venus,
which of course we didn't know or think of as the mount of
    Venus.
And on this too there seemed to be a wet patch.
Was she thinking of Mr Knight?
As she sat there in mild exhibitionism.

Prep Schools all move in a mysterious way.

Epithalamion for George MacBeth and Penny Church

The epithalamia are so many!
(though,
when I was married, I didn't have any).

Thousands! and so
I'm a little shy of adding to the score –
perhaps the Muse won't want to hear any more?

But George is a very classical person –
he
won't mind if I voice or verse an
elegant wee
Anglo-Scottish odd kind of ode –
it's a way of sending love and good wishes in code.

And most surely the Muse must like Penny?
and,
from Aberdeen to Abergavenny,
know that the hand
best suited to be taken in marriage
is hers? So I retract my undercarriage

and take off boldly! The empyrean
seems
full of Byronic Assyrian
erotic dreams –
I'm sure they'll live there happily!
Blissful as the *lazzaroni** in Napoli!

---

* The *lazzaroni* (criminal layabouts) of Naples are traditionally supposed to
lead a carefree and untrammelled existence.

Haiku of a British Soldier Who Has Had Dysentery in India

My arse'ole felt like
it was somewhere up 'ere, mate,
round my fucking neck!

Miss Print Writes an Old-Fashioned Romantic Novel

His voice stank to a whisper:
'He's the greatest villain unhinged!'
She scarcely regarded him but went on packing a shitcase.
When she next designed to look at him, it was in a very
    unpeasant way.
'*Merde alors!*' she rasped.
'Like Burgess and Maclean, he is a defecator!' . . .

He held her tight. 'You are so lively!' he murmured.
'I adorn you!' Her slender young figure . . . her hops . . . her
    graceful lambs . . .
'You are like a great big boar!' She goggled delightedly . . .

There stood an old crane. Her hair was grey and waspy.
She who had once been the Madam of the bethel at Amiens!
And now no truce of her pervious beauty . . .

Cross Words

Palimpsestic imbrication
makes the critics hot,
legends, myths and transcendentals
and the What Is Not –

at the Court, where sweet Ophelia
has fits of the glums,
Antony and Cleopatra
kiss each others' tums.

Simple things aren't for the learnèd –
there's one single crime:
taking time out from the scholars'
crossword puzzle time!

Tales From Isherwood Forest

In the land of Homophobia
there was verdant claustrophobia,
all the boys were greenly conscious
that the trees were at their elbows –
they were in the forest, hiding,
in that Thirties forest hiding
all their impulses and passions,
exiled from Society, hiding . . .

Forest birds were singing Weill songs,
Wandervogel Berlin Weill songs,

Mack the Knife and green of hunters –
wanderers they were and bowmen,
high-class homosexual hunters.
No suspender-belts or women,
all was clean and pure in Nature,
nothing bad like menstruation
stained the radiance of their lifestyle . . .
it was venison and drinking,
hunting through the glades and cruising
down the tree-lined rides of pleasure.
Buggery and masturbation
and the sweet delights of leather!
Sunburned brown in *lederhosen*,
all of them had been to Salzburg,
Munich too – but Berlin mostly.
Drinking wine from leather goblets,
cold white wine in lake-cooled bottles,
leather flasks too, medieval!
With their knives they hacked the stagmeat,
singing little chunks of Wagner –
Issyvoo was in his glory,
there were campfire tales of Wystan,
Public Lavatories and policemen . . .

Brotherly, the sexual sagas
wore away the nescient nightwood –
tales of all the woods of England
and the Chiemsee Bar in Salzburg,
hunting, searching, questful nomads,
in all ways the Quest was honoured,
with the Prize of hands and kisses.
Sages talked of paedophilia,
blackboard chalk and paedophilia,
pupils promising and pretty –
toasts were drunk to Guy and Brian . . .

Venison and fish and berries,
sex and song. Immortal diet –

so they very clearly thought it.
Persecuted? Yes, but cosy!
Happy in that daylong, nightlong
green primeval psychic forest!

Sir Arthur Sullivan's Nightmare Song

(Tune from *The Yeomen Of The Guard*)

The cock may twist and the rump may turn
and boys may bleed and desires may burn
and the late-night suppers that please the Prince
may make Morality into mince!

In chambres separées with the flirting fan
the ticklish vulva admits a man,
satins and silks, and the night-time cats
are mistresses of aristocrats!

Champagne may pop and the feet entwine
and lips may open for more than wine
and in male brothels the eyes grow fond
as I write hymns for the demi-monde!

The Influence of D. H. Lawrence on the Language of Gardeners and Gamekeepers in the Thirties

O hear the dreadful C-word
that makes the lilies faint!
While F-words in the greenhouse,
they fairly strip the paint!

The intercourse invoked is
what turns the roses blue!
Varieties of loving
all quite unknown at Kew!

The lightest of the pinks – all
go deepest red with shame!
The things they've never thought of
are mentioned now by name!

And in the rides where pheasants
have never heard of sex
or pondered on the rabbits,
it makes them nervous wrecks!

The foxes and the badgers
go round with knowing looks –
their innocence has vanished
through sophisticated books!

Like Adam in the garden,
the time he fell for Eve,
a novel's altered everything
in a way you'd not believe!

The Cleverness of Clark

Don't let the fact ever escape me!
Oh, let it escape me never
   that Clark is clever!
Know, while the summer sun shines
and the winter's rainy,
   that Clark is brainy!

This is not a topic for humour,
to make comments lax or lewd on,
   Clark's head is screwed on!
As sure as God made toffee apples
and old tramps have bunions,
   Clark knows his onions!

Born yesterday he wasn't,
he knows for sure what's whattish,
   Clark isn't sottish!
I'll bet an Old Wellingtonian tie
and several pairs of my boots –
   that Clark's a slyboots!

He can't be circumvented
or easily caught – like a fish by an angler –
   Clark's a Senior Wrangler,
compared to me! Clark rings the bell,
he can tinkle a zing or two –
   Clark knows a thing or two!

An Ogden Nash for Julian Symons

The characters in the English detective stories of the
  Twenties and Thirties
are all clean-livers. There are no dirties.
They never seem to eat – there are no long descriptions of
  meals and such –
and it doesn't look as though they drink very much.
Though occasionally perhaps one of them is an old soak
and (funnily enough, in this Puritan atmosphere) some of
  them smoke.

They never go to the loo. There's no record of that.
They don't masturbate either. Their lives are flat.
Though there may be adultery and fornication,
what they actually *do* is left to your imagination.
They *can* work in offices; but most have English County
  week-ends.
And some, in every book, are destined to meet very bleak
  ends.
Shot or knifed or pushed down a spiral staircase –
or cunningly poisoned (that's by no means a rare case).

They may gaze at lovely landscapes, bathed in the evening
  sun –
but when you come to reckon it up, they don't have very
  much *fun*.
They wear no underclothes. There's no mention of
  knickers –
the light of sexual interest never even flickers –
there are no tits, or erections, or sensual thighs;
though a girl, quite often, can have beautiful eyes . . .

So if you want to be well-fed, wined and dined – or
  flirty . . .
don't be a character in an English detective story of
  (around) 1920 or 1930!